Spanish Missionaries

A Proud Heritage The Hispanic Library

Spanish Missionaries

Bringing Spanish Culture to the Americas

R. Conrad Stein

Content Adviser: Dr. John Kessell
Historian
University of New Mexico
Albuquerque, New Mexico

Published in the United States of America by The Child's World®
PO Box 326 • Chanhassen, MN 55317-0326 • 800-599-READ • www.childsworld.com

Acknowledgments
   The Child's World®: Mary Berendes, Publishing Director
   Editorial Directions, Inc.: E. Russell Primm, Editorial Director; Pam Rosenberg, Project
   Editor; Katie Marsico, Associate Editor; Matt Messbarger, Editorial Assistant; Susan Hindman,
   Copyeditor; Susan Ashley, Proofreader; Molly Symmonds, Fact Checker; Timothy Griffin/
   IndexServ, Indexer; Dawn Friedman, Photo Researcher; Linda S. Koutris, Photo Selector

   Creative Spark: Mary Francis and Rob Court, Design and Page Production

   Cartography by XNR Productions, Inc.

Photos
   Cover: church of the Mission San Xavier del Bac, near Tucson, Arizona, Buddy Mays/Corbis

   Architect of the Capitol, U.S. Capitol, Washington, DC: 22; Cameraphoto Arte, Venice/Art
   Resource, NY: 12; Erich Lessing/Art Resource, NY: 36; G.E. Kidder Smith/Corbis: 8; Christie's
   Images/Corbis: 14; Wolfgang Kaehler/Corbis: 16; Corbis: 20, 26; Michael Freeman/Corbis:
   23; Joel W. Rogers/Corbis: 27; Robert Holmes/Corbis: 28; D. Boone/Corbis: 32; Ted
   Streshinsky/Corbis: 34; Bettmann/Corbis: 35; The Granger Collection, New York: 10, 19, 29,
   31; N. Walker/North Wind Picture Archives: 7, 15; North Wind Picture Archives: 11, 13, 17,
   21; Stock Montage, Inc.: 9, 33.

Registration

Library of Congress Cataloging-in-Publication Data
   Stein, R. Conrad.
      Spanish missionaries : bringing Spanish culture to the Americas / by R. Conrad Stein.
         p. cm. — (A proud heritage)
      Includes bibliographical references and index.
      ISBN 1-59296-387-0 (Library Bound : alk. paper) 1. Missions, Spanish—Southwest, New—
   History—Juvenile literature. 2. Spaniards—Southwest, New—History—Juvenile literature. 3.
   Indians of North America—Missions—Southwest, New—History—Juvenile literature. 4.
   Southwest, New—History—To 1848—Juvenile literature. I. Title. II. Proud heritage (Child's
   World (Firm))
   F799.S74 2005
   978'.01—dc22   2004018049

New Mexico: Motherland of the American West

"Thanks be to God. I arrived here at the port of San Diego. It is beautiful to behold . . ."

(Father Junípero Serra, 1769)

In 1598, a wealthy Spanish miner named Don Juan de Oñate led a group of colonists out of Mexico and into the little-known lands to the north. Nearly 80 years earlier, Spanish adventurers had conquered the Aztec people of Mexico and **plundered** their gold and silver. This led Don Juan de Oñate to believe that a fortune awaited him to the north, in the region called New Mexico. He was wrong. New Mexico contained no mines. Instead, Oñate fought a war with the Native American people of New Mexico. He returned to Mexico without ever finding the silver he hungered for.

Don Juan de Oñate wrote this inscription along an old Spanish trail in western New Mexico. It notes that he passed this way on April 16, 1605.

Although their leader had resigned, Oñate's colonists stayed in New Mexico. They were mostly farmers who looked to New Mexico as an inviting land where they could establish farms, villages, and churches. Among them were a group of men known as missionaries. They were devoted to a single mission, a **divine** purpose in life. The missionaries lived to bring Christianity to the people of the Americas.

The San José de la Laguna Mission was built between 1699 and 1701. It is located near Albuquerque, New Mexico.

The Spanish missionaries in what became the American West were Catholic priests. They built churches and schools and taught European methods of farming. Many modern historians look past these contributions, however, and regard the missionaries as invaders—trespassers on Native American soil. It is true that missionaries sometimes forced their religion upon the Native Americans. But the mission priests were far gentler than the goldseekers and soldiers who first marched into the western regions. The priests

In 1521, the bold Spanish soldier Hernando Cortés conquered the Aztec people of central Mexico and established a vast colony called New Spain. The colony stretched north from Panama to what is now the southwestern part of the United States. The region north of the Rio Grande came to be known as New Spain's northern frontier. The northern frontier spread over present-day Texas, New Mexico, Arizona, Colorado, Utah, Nevada, and California. At first, this vast region was Spanish in name only because it contained few Spanish settlements. Over time, the Spanish influence became stronger, as dedicated missionaries and colonists settled the land.

The Pilgrims land at Plymouth Rock, Massachusetts, in 1620.

carried no swords or firearms. Their weapon was the Christian cross.

In 1610, Spanish settlers founded the city of Santa Fe in what today is the state of New Mexico. Schools in the United States often teach that American history began in the East when Pilgrims from England established their settlement at Plymouth, Massachusetts, in 1620. In fact, Santa Fe was settled 10 years before Plymouth.

From Santa Fe, missionaries spread throughout New Mexico and beyond. These men of the Christian God discovered two types of Native American people in the region. The first were farmers who lived in permanent villages. The priests called the farming people *Pueblos,* from the Spanish word meaning "town." The other Native Americans lived by hunting and were nomads, meaning they had no settled villages.

Spanish settlers in New Mexico had much in common with the Pueblos. Both farmed for a living, and they learned readily from each other. Spaniards brought wheat to the American West. The Pueblos aided the Spaniards in growing their **staple** food, corn. Spaniards and Pueblos developed a common enemy in the nomads. For generations, the nomads had raided Pueblo fields for food. Now, Spanish settlers fought side by side with the Pueblos

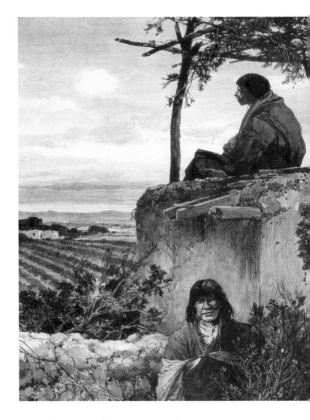

Pueblo Indians watch over their fields in New Mexico. Corn was an important part of the Pueblo diet.

against the raiders. Pueblos called the nomadic tribes *apachu* (enemy) and *apachu nabahu* (enemy of farmers' fields). From these words came the tribal names Apache and Navajo. In later years, the Apaches and the Navajos would prove to be among the fiercest fighters in the American West.

A majority of Spanish missionaries on the northern frontier were members of a Catholic group of priests known as the Franciscans. The group was founded in the early 1200s by Saint Francis of Assisi. Francis was born into a wealthy family in the town of Assisi in Italy. As a young man, he **renounced** his family's wealth and made a vow to live in poverty. Patterning himself after Jesus, he traveled among poor people, tending to the sick and preaching the Christian Gospel. His followers, the Franciscan priests, also

Francesco di Pietro di Bernardone, more commonly known as Saint Francis of Assisi, was born in 1181 or 1182 and died in 1226.

Priests, soldiers, and Native Americans all lived together in Spanish missions in North America.

rejected wealth. In the Americas, they often went hungry. They frequently faced death at the hands of Native Americans, who regarded them as invaders.

By 1630, the mission priests had built dozens of churches in New Mexico. Some learned the languages of the Pueblo people and taught the Indians basic Spanish. Each village had at least one church. Churches served both the Spanish settlers and the Pueblo Indians. Most of the settlers came from Mexico and were members of the new *mestizo* race. Mestizo people have both European and Native American ancestors. Today, the majority of Mexicans are mestizos.

Despite the missionaries' work in the villages, Spanish settlers clashed with their Native American neighbors. Religion often lay at the heart of their

Mission Storytelling

The missionaries discovered that the Pueblos loved story-telling. This worked in their favor since the Bible contains a wealth of stories. Priests staged plays that were attended by settlers as well as Pueblos. The tale of Adam and Eve was always popular. A prop onstage stood for the Tree of Good and Evil. Young boys and girls served as actors. Members of the audience gasped and squirmed in their seats as the girl playing Eve offered Adam the forbidden fruit. When Adam accepted the apple, the people sighed, knowing that humanity was now kicked out of Eden and condemned to suffering.

disputes. In New Mexico, mission priests forbade Pueblo men and women to worship their old gods. The priests' authority was enforced by armed Spaniards. Pueblo people who continued their old religious practices were subjected to punishment. On occasion, they were whipped or even hung for the crime of witchcraft.

In 1680, a Pueblo leader named Popé led a rebellion against the priests and the Spanish soldiers. Popé claimed the

A drawing of a thunderbird with lightening and rain appears on a Pueblo wall in New Mexico. Native Americans in missions were not allowed to worship their old gods.

ancient gods had given him special powers. During a bloody religious war, more than 400 settlers were killed and dozens of churches were destroyed. Popé set himself up as the leader of all the Pueblos, but life was not much better under Popé's leadership. When Popé died, the Spaniards took control of Pueblo lands once again.

During the Pueblo Revolt, Spanish settlers fled Santa Fe and took refuge near what is now El Paso, Texas. Every day, they prayed to a small wooden statue of the Virgin Mary, imploring her to let them return to their homes. They prayed for 12 long years. Finally, in 1693, the Pueblo War ended and the settlers were allowed back in Santa Fe. The same wooden statue of the Virgin Mary now stands in Santa Fe's Saint Francis Cathedral (above). Today, the statue is called Our Lady of Peace and some people pray to it in the hope of bringing peace to the world.

New Mexico became the most heavily populated province on New Spain's northern frontier. By 1800, Santa Fe, Albuquerque, and other towns were well established. Almost all of New Mexico's Pueblo people had become Christians. But nomadic tribes, including the Navajos and the Apaches, still resisted the new religion.

A Santa Fe scene shows what a street in the town may have looked like in the early 1800s.

Chapter Two

The Mission Movement in Texas and Arizona

Early Spanish explorers entering what is now the American Southwest met a Native American tribe whose word for friends was *tejas*. From this word, the Spaniards chose Texas as the name for the province east of New Mexico. In 1682, Spanish missionaries built the first two Catholic churches in Texas at a site near present-day El Paso. The Spaniards introduced cattle to the province, and Texas gained fame as cattle country.

In 1718, a Franciscan priest named Olivares founded a church at what is now San Antonio, Texas. At first, the church was called Mission San Antonio de Valero. Later, the church was named the Alamo after a Spanish word describing a nearby grove of cottonwood trees. In 1836, the Alamo was the scene of a terrible battle that eventually led to the American takeover of New Spain's northern frontier.

Hollywood movies have long celebrated the lingo, or special language, of Texas cowboys. The movies rarely mention that cowboy talk comes from Spanish. When Americans from the East arrived in Texas, they found Mexican *vaqueros* (cowboys) working on ranches. The Americans quickly picked up vaquero terms. A fenced-in cattle pen was called a corral after a Spanish word of that spelling. The cowboys roped cattle with a lasso, which is derived from the Spanish word *lazo,* meaning "noose." A cowboy who knew the ways of a ranch well was said to be savvy, from the Spanish word *saber* (to know). All these terms were part of the colorful cowboy lingo.

Military forts and mission churches were often built side by side on New Spain's northern frontier. Forts and the soldiers inside them protected the churches from Native American raiding parties. But there was also a hidden purpose in the cooperation between the missions and the military. The Spanish government looked to the mission movement to expand and defend Spanish territory.

The government of Spain needed more citizens in the Americas. Therefore, Spain hoped the missionaries

Spanish forts such as the Presidio in modern-day San Francisco, California, helped protect Spain's settlements on the northern frontier.

would teach Native Americans to worship like Spaniards, farm like Spaniards, speak like Spaniards, and dress like Spaniards. In this manner, the Native American people would eventually become Spanish citizens. As loyal Spaniards, they would protect their land from any foreign country—including the ever-ambitious United States. Most missionaries, however, were **pious** men. The priests believed their first duty

A Spanish missionary preaches to Native Americans in California.

was to preach the Gospel, not to mold Native Americans into Spanish citizens.

One such dedicated missionary was Father Eusebio Francisco Kino (1645–1711). As a teenager, Kino was stricken with a deadly illness. In prayers, he promised God that if he recovered, he would devote his life to

Father Kino became a Jesuit in 1665 and was sent to Mexico City as a missionary in 1681.

the priesthood. He got well, and he fulfilled his vow. Father Kino differed from most other missionaries in New Spain. He was Italian, not Spanish. He was also a member of the Jesuit religious order, while most of his fellow priests were Franciscans. Kino was kind to the Native Americans in the Southwest, and they returned his kindness. He often clashed with Spanish authorities because he refused to force Christianity on his followers.

Father Kino was one of the first priests to venture into what is now the state of Arizona. He explored the desert and the mountain regions and discovered an ancient network of canals used hundreds of years earlier by a mysterious Native American group called the Hohokam. With the help of Native American workers, he founded ranches and brought water to parched desert land. Kino established many mission communities in southern Arizona and northern Mexico. He started farms and cattle ranches, which eventually fed thousands of people. Today, a statue of Father Kino stands in the U.S. Capitol in Washington, D.C. The statue proudly represents the state of Arizona.

Father Eusebio Francisco Kino laid the foundation of the first church at San Xavier del Bac Mission in 1700. Construction of the church that still stands at the mission (below) was begun in 1783.

Chapter Three

California Missions

California was the most remote province on New Spain's northern frontier. The land route from Mexico to California stretched over forbidding mountains, waterless deserts, and hostile Native American territory. Because of its isolation, the mission system was slow to develop in California.

The Spanish priest Junípero Serra (1713–1784) had the greatest impact on early California history. Father Serra sailed to Mexico from Spain in 1749. Soon after arriving, he was bitten on the left leg by a snake or an insect. The bite never healed properly. For the rest of his life, he walked with a painful limp. Yet Serra became known as the "walking friar," because he journeyed thousands of miles on foot doing his missionary work.

In 1769, Father Serra arrived at what is now San Diego, California. Immediately he set to work building

Spanish Missionaries traveled throughout the American Southwest trying to convert Native Americans to Christianity.

California's first mission church. That church was a humble structure made of logs with mud used as plaster. The church had a bell that Father Serra rang to summon the Native Americans to worship. It was the first in a series of remarkable mission churches built by Spanish priests in California.

By 1823, Spaniards had constructed a series of 21 missions along the California coast. Each church was about a day's walk from the other. Like links on a long chain, the churches stretched from San Diego north to San Francisco. Trading posts and thriving farming communities grew around the mission churches in Spanish California. The churches were connected by what the Spaniards called the *Camino Real,* or "Royal Road." During the mission era, the Royal Road was

The Missions Today

Today, the 21 Spanish mission churches are the pride of California. The churches and their grounds have been magnificently restored. Millions of tourists come to the missions each year to marvel at the pioneering work accomplished by Spanish priests. Pots, pans, and utensils used by cooks are displayed in the kitchens of some missions. Original carpentry tools and farm implements are also preserved. A visit to any of the California missions is like opening a door to the past.

nothing more than a muddy footpath. Many years later, it became California's famous Highway 101.

California's Highway 101 follows the same route as the Camino Real of the Spanish settlers.

California's mission churches stir controversy as well as wonder. Were these wonderful structures built by free Christian people, or were they constructed with what amounted to slave labor? Each mission church employed hundreds, maybe even thousands, of Native American workers. The workers were required to be baptized into Christianity. Newly baptized Native Americans were called neophytes. The neophytes could be whipped or put in chains if they disobeyed their superiors. They were forced to live in cramped barracks where diseases spread rapidly among them. One priest wrote, "[The Indians] live well free but as soon as

The San Buenaventura Mission in Ventura, California, was the last mission founded by Father Junípero Serra. Founded in 1782, the mission's church still serves as a Catholic house of worship.

we reduce them to a Christian and community life . . . they sicken and die."

Father Serra founded nine mission churches and personally baptized more than 5,000 Native Americans. He taught reading, carpentry, metalworking, and farming skills. But he and fellow priests apparently believed that an occasional beating discouraged sin and helped the Indians get into heaven. In 1780, Serra wrote, "Spiritual fathers should punish their sons, the Indians, with blows."

Mission San Francisco de Asis, commonly known as Mission Dolores, was founded in 1776 under the direction of Father Junípero Serra.

Today, Father Serra's statue stands in San Francisco's Golden Gate Park. Historians often hail Father Serra as a brave California pioneer. But many Native American groups regard Serra as a shameful figure rather than a hero in California history.

Chapter Four

The End of the Mission Era

In 1821, Mexican patriots overthrew Spanish rule and established an independent nation. The new government did not support the work of Catholic missionaries. In the 1830s, missions on the northern frontier were broken up, and the land was sold to private farmers. Sales of mission land officially ended the work of missionary priests on Mexico's northern frontier.

The northern frontier soon experienced a far more profound change. By the 1820s, only about 40,000 settlers from Mexico lived above the Rio Grande under the Mexican flag. This sparse population made the area a tempting target for Mexico's neighbor, the United States. Land-hungry American farmers flooded into Texas and quickly outnumbered Mexican settlers there. In 1836, the Americans fought a ferocious battle with the Mexican army at the Alamo, the old mission

Father Miguel Hidalgo calls for Mexicans to revolt against Spain in 1810. He is known as the Father of Mexican Independence.

The building that became known as the Alamo was originally the chapel of the Mission San Antonio de Valero in San Antonio, Texas.

church in San Antonio. The Americans later proclaimed Texas to be an independent nation.

Then, in the 1840s, the idea of manifest destiny began to excite the American people. Those who believed in manifest destiny insisted the United States should expand its territory from the East Coast to the West Coast. It made no difference that Mexico claimed the regions from Texas to California. Manifest destiny was looked upon almost as a commandment issued by God.

Disputes over territory triggered the Mexican War, which was fought between the United States and Mexico from 1846 to 1848. The war proved to be a disaster for Mexico. The Mexican government was forced to **cede** almost its entire northern frontier to the United States. With the end of the Mexican War, manifest destiny

In 1847, during the Mexican War, U.S. soldiers stormed the hill of Chapultepec as they marched toward Mexico City.

Mission San Antonio de Padua was founded by Father Junípero Serra in 1771.

was complete. The United States stretched from the Atlantic Ocean to the Pacific Ocean, from sea to shining sea.

The Spanish missionary movement in the American West is now remembered as history. Not all historians look kindly upon the work of the missionaries. The mission priests were **zealous** in their desire to erase old religious beliefs from the minds of Native Americans and replace them with Christian ideals. Sometimes the priests used cruel methods to bring Christianity to the people. Still, mission farms gave Native Americans a far better food supply than they'd had in the past. Also, many Native Americans became **devout** Christians.

Not all Native Americans willingly accepted Christianity. Spanish missionaries sometimes forced them to accept this new religion.

Historians argue about the contributions—both positive and negative—made by Spanish missionaries. But all agree the missionaries were brave men who wrote a vital chapter in the history of the American West.

A Spanish missionary wrote this book detailing mission life.

Timeline

1521: Hernando Cortés conquers the Aztecs and establishes the empire of New Spain.

1630: Led by missionaries, the Pueblo Indians have built dozens of churches in New Mexico.

1645: Father Eusebio Francisco Kino is born on August 10.

1680: Chief Popé leads the Pueblo people into war against the Spanish settlers and the missionaries.

1682: Mission priests build the first two churches in Texas.

1691: Father Eusebio Francisco Kino begins his missionary work in Arizona.

1693: The Pueblo War ends, and Spanish settlers return to Santa Fe.

1713: Junipero Serra is born on November 24.

1718: A mission church later called the Alamo is built in San Antonio, Texas.

1769: Father Junípero Serra arrives in San Diego, California, and immediately begins to build the first of California's 21 mission churches.

1821: Mexican patriots break from Spanish rule and establish an independent nation.

1836: Americans living in Texas fight the Mexican army at the Battle of the Alamo.

1846–1848: The United States and Mexico wage war; after the Mexican War, the government of Mexico cedes most of its northern frontier to the United States.

cede (SEED) To cede territory is to give it up, usually as a result of a war. The Mexican government was forced to cede almost its entire northern frontier to the United States.

devout (di-VOWT) A person who is devout is deeply religious and devoted to his faith. Many Native Americans became devout Christians.

divine (duh-VINE) Something that is divine has to do with God. Missionaries believed that converting people to Christianity was their divine purpose in life.

pious (PYE-uhs) A person who practices his or her religion with great faith and seriousness is said to be pious. Most missionaries were pious men.

plundered (PLUHN-durd) If something is plundered, it is stolen with the use of force. Spanish adventurers conquered the Aztec people of Mexico and plundered their gold and silver.

renounced (re-NOUNSD) To renounce something is to give it up. Saint Francis of Assisi renounced his family's wealth and made a vow to live in poverty.

staple (STAY-puhl) A staple crop is the main crop that is grown in a particular region. The Pueblos aided the Spaniards in growing corn, their staple food.

zealous (ZEL-uhs) To be zealous is to be full of eagerness and enthusiasm. The mission priests were zealous in their desire to erase old religious beliefs from the minds of Native Americans and replace them with Christian ideals.

Books

Bowler, Sarah. *Father Junípero Serra and the California Missions*. Chanhassen, Minn.: The Child's World, 2003.

Gaines, Ann. *The Alamo: The Fight over Texas*. Chanhassen, Minn.: The Child's World, 2003.

Keremitsis, Eileen. *Life in a California Mission*. New York: Lucent Books, 2002.

Staeger, Rob. *The Spanish Missions of California*. Broomall, Penn.: Mason Crest Publishers, 2002.

Web Sites

Visit our home page for lots of links about Spanish missionaries:

http://www.childsworld.com/links.html

Note to Parents, Teachers, and Librarians:
We routinely check our Web links to make sure they're safe, active sites—
so encourage your readers to check them out!

About the Author

R. Conrad Stein was born in Chicago. At age 18, he joined the Marine Corps and served for three years. He later attended the University of Illinois, where he graduated with a degree in history. A full-time writer, Mr. Stein has published more than 100 books for young readers. He lived in Mexico for many years, and his family still vacations in that country. The author now lives in Chicago with his wife (children's book author Deborah Kent) and their daughter, Janna.